WHY DON'T ELEPHANTS LIVE IN THE CITY?

By Katherine Smith

Consultant: Nicola Davies

KU-226-329

ticktock
MEDIA

WHY DON'T ELEPHANTS LIVE IN THE CITY?

Laois Co
Leabh...............laois
Acc. No. ...06/...865
Class No. 599.67
Inv. No. 8932

WITHDRAWN FROM STOCK

Copyright © *ticktock* Entertainment Ltd 2004
First published in Great Britain in 2004 by *ticktock* Media Ltd.,
Unit 2, Orchard Business Centre, North Farm Road, Tunbridge Wells, Kent, TN2 3XF
We would like to thank: Meme Ltd and Elizabeth Wiggans.
ISBN 1 86007 516 9 PB
ISBN 1 86007 520 7 HB
Printed in China
A CIP catalogue record for this book is available from the British Library.
All rights reserved. No part of this publication may be reproduced,
copied, stored in a retrieval system, or transmitted in any form or by
any means electronic, mechanical, photocopying, recording or otherwise
without prior written permission of the copyright owner.

CONTENTS

Any words appearing in the text in bold, **like this**, are explained in the Glossary.

Why don't elephants
live in the city?

4

Because elephants are the biggest land mammals on Earth, and they need lots of space!

Elephants live in family groups, called **herds**. They roam the hot grasslands, forests, marshes, and deserts of Africa and Asia where there is plenty of room to move around!

There are usually about eight females, their young, and one male **bull elephant** in a herd.

Elephants share grasslands with zebras, giraffes, and rhinos.

African elephants have dips in their backs, and are bigger than Asian elephants.

Human beings are the elephant's only **predator!**

Bull elephants often live in male-only herds or on their own.

Why don't elephants have small noses?

Because elephants need their long trunks to do lots of clever things!

An elephant's **trunk** is actually its nose and top lip joined together. But the trunk is used for much more than smelling! Think of all the ways you use your hands – to pick things up, to scratch your head, to touch, to hold, and to move things. Elephants use their trunks for all these tasks and many more!

An elephant can use its trunk like a hose, to suck up and squirt water.

Elephants make loud trumpeting sounds with their long trunks.

Elephants can also use their trunks to breathe above water while they are swimming.

An adult African elephant's trunk is about 2 metres long.

Why don't elephants have small ears?

Because elephants use their big ears to fan themselves in the heat.

Elephants also swim to cool off. They protect their skin from biting insects and sunburn by squirting water over their backs!

Elephants have long eyelashes to protect their eyes.

When facing danger, bull elephants stretch out their ears to make themselves look bigger and more threatening.

Every elephant's ears are unique. No two are alike.

Researchers believe elephants have good hearing and can "talk" to each other from far away.

Why don't elephants have smooth skin?

Because elephants need skin that bends and moves.

Imagine how hard it would be to bend your thumb without the stretchy wrinkles around the knuckle. Elephants are huge. Their skin needs to be really baggy and stretchy so that they can move easily.

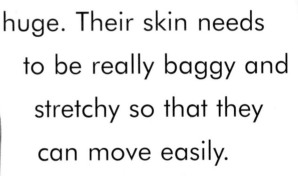

Elephants are born with wrinkled skin.

Young elephants are born with a fine coat of hair that protects their skin from sunburn.

Elephants have big, padded feet to support their enormous weight. This stops them from sinking into the ground.

Elephants have four thick legs. They support the elephant's massive body.

Why don't elephants have lots of calves at once?

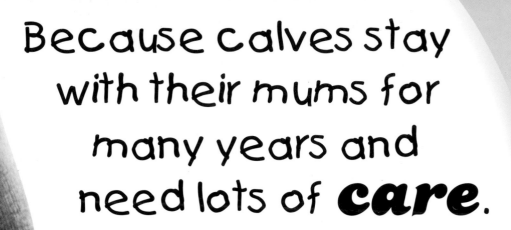

Because calves stay with their mums for many years and need lots of **care**.

Elephants usually have only one calf every three or four years. When a **calf** is born, it can stand and feed milk from its mother within a few hours.

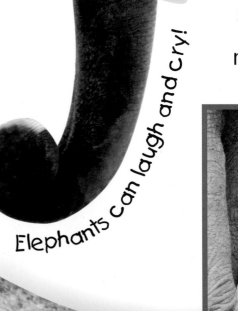

Elephants can laugh and cry!

The entire herd help to look after the calf. They even comfort it with a cuddle when it is hurt or sad.

Soon after a calf is born, the other elephants in the herd come to welcome it.

It takes time for the young calf to learn to use its trunk.

Baby elephants even suck their trunks like a big thumb!

Young elephants stay close to their mothers until they are about ten years old.

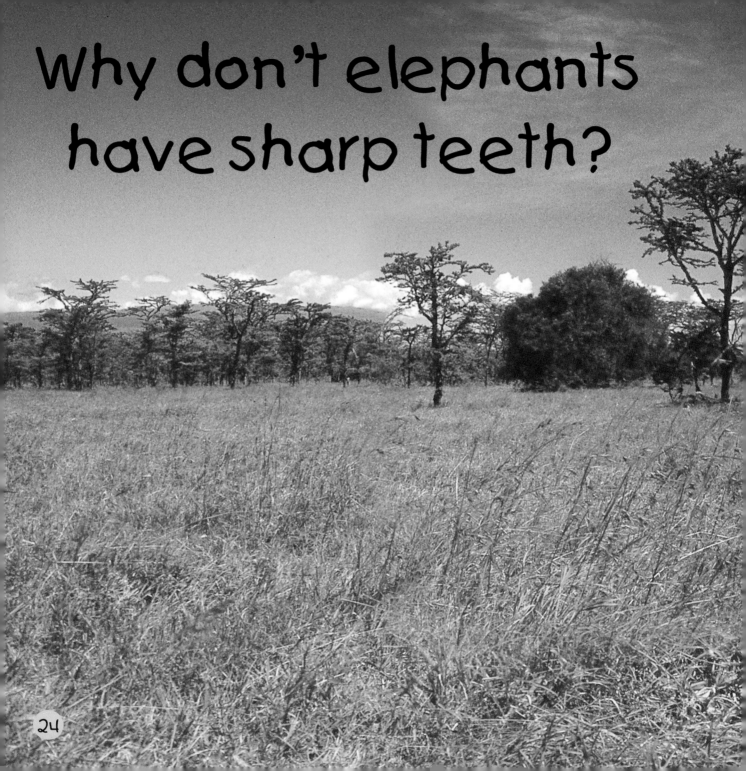

Why don't elephants have sharp teeth?

Because elephants are herbivores, and don't need sharp teeth.

Elephants eat mainly leaves, grass, fruit, twigs, bark, and roots. They have four large teeth called **molars**, for chewing and grinding up this tough food. Their **tusks** are really very long front teeth, which they use for digging up roots and peeling off tree bark.

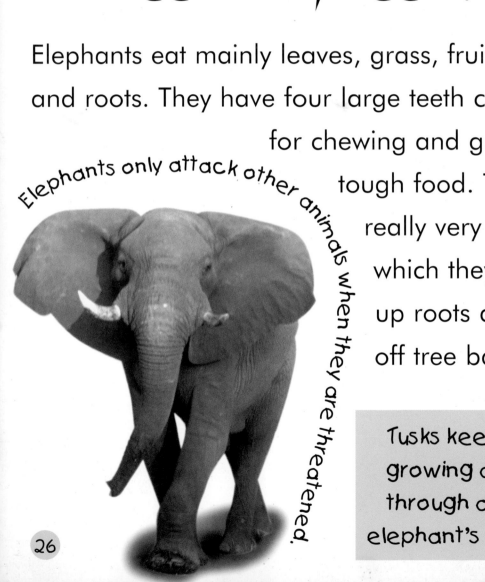

Elephants only attack other animals when they are threatened.

Tusks keep growing all through an elephant's life.

Elephants often break down trees in their search for food.

Each molar weighs as much as a brick!

Elephant PROFILE

Life span

70 years.

Size

3–4 metres tall. That's nearly twice as tall as a man!

Weight

An adult male weighs 5,900 kilograms, which is more than four cars!

Numbers

There are estimated to be 300,000 to 600,000 African elephants and 35,000 to 50,000 Asian elephants.

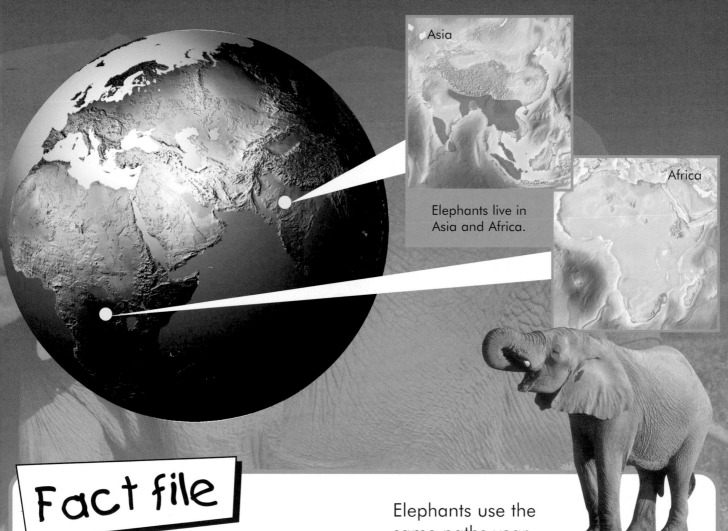

Asia

Africa

Elephants live in
Asia and Africa.

Fact file

Elephants can breathe through
their trunks when they swim.

Elephants eat up to 454 kilograms
of food in a day and drink 110–190
litres of water.

Elephants use the
same paths year
after year as they
march across the wide, open
spaces looking for food and water.

Elephants make waterholes in dry
riverbeds. Other animals use these
waterholes as well.

29

GLOSSARY

Bull elephant — The name for an adult male elephant.

Calf — The name for a baby elephant. It is also used for the young of cattle, whales, and other animals.

Herds — Groups of animals that live and eat together.

Mammals — Animals that are warm-blooded and produce milk for their young.

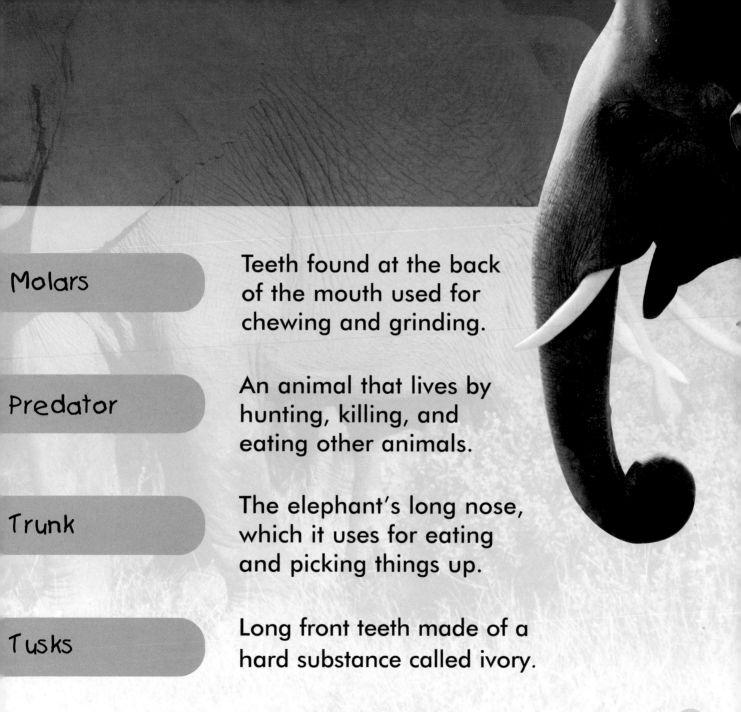

Molars — Teeth found at the back of the mouth used for chewing and grinding.

Predator — An animal that lives by hunting, killing, and eating other animals.

Trunk — The elephant's long nose, which it uses for eating and picking things up.

Tusks — Long front teeth made of a hard substance called ivory.

INDEX